ILLUSTRATED
EDITION!

**DAD
JOKES**

HIGHLY
CONCENTRATED
DAD HUMOR

Producer & International Distributor
eBookPro Publishing
www.ebook-pro.com

Dad Jokes
Random Mouse

Content: Random Mouse, Arbel Singer
Cover Design & Illustrations: Maria Sokhatski

Contact: agency@ebook-pro.com
ISBN 9798398180367

So you got a new Dad Jokes book for...

☑ **Father's day**

☑ **Christmas**

☑ **Birthday**

☑ **Thanksgiving**

Quick, say something grateful
and sincere!

Look, we know that if you're reading this, chances are you don't *need* help telling (obviously) hilarious knee-slappers that'll make families tear up instantly – you're the best dad anyone could ever wish for!

But if you did get this book, it means someone in your family or close friends cares about you and wants you to enjoy life, keep everyone laughing, and be the glue that holds the family together.

... or they want you to update your repertoire. You know, even Muhamad Ali needed some coaching every once in a while.

We sat, brainstormed, channeled ancient dad wisdom, and gathered 200 hilarious jokes you *probably* haven't heard before. So, we hope that you use them to make your loved ones smile, cry, and regret ever giving you this book.

Sincerely
Random mouse

I tried to teach my dog to
get a stick from a mile away,

•••

**BUT IT WAS TOO
FAR-FETCHED.**

Did you hear about the new
"constipation" movie?

•••

IT HASN'T COME OUT YET.

I got harassed at the
Renaissance fair.

•••

**GOOD THING I BROUGHT
MY MACE.**

How do spacemen
tie their shoes?

•••

WITH AN ASTRO-KNOT.

Why did lightning leave
the party early?

•••

HE HAD TO BOLT.

You're really gonna ask
linguini out?

•••

**I HEARD IT WAS
PASTA ROUND.**

Why was the impatient
bodybuilder disqualified
from the tournament?

•••

**HE COULDN'T HANDLE
THE WAIT.**

Did you hear about the DJ
who broke his back?

•••

SLIPPED HIS DISC.

What did Kanye name
his model car?

•••

KIM CARDASHIAN.

I spilled ketchup on
my new socks.

•••

**IT WENT STRAIGHT
TOMATOES.**

Why are there only 25 letters
in the queen's alphabet?

•••

SHE DRANK ALL THE T.

I dropped some mean bars
while sitting on the toilet.

•••

I CALL IT CRAP MUSIC.

Did you hear about the African mammal with a skin condition and a drinking problem?

•••

THE NEW ALBINO WINO RHINO.

The police are looking for a fortune-telling midget.

•••

THE WARRANT IS FOR A SMALL MEDIUM AT LARGE.

I got into a fight with
a former president.

•••

**I TOTALLY GOT
BUSH-WACKED.**

The guy who used to sell
chowder around the corner
went to jail.

•••

**I HOPE HE DOESN'T
DROP THE SOUP.**

Which shape works best
for repelling witches?

•••

HEX-A-GONE.

Mommy, why didn't Santa
bring me my gift?

•••

**– BECAUSE OF THE RAIN,
DEAR.**

The hotdog-eating competition
ran out of food.

•••

THERE WAS NO WIENER.

Why does nobody like
the class goldfish?

•••

HE'S THE TEACHER'S PET.

All the children in class
fell asleep.

•••

**THEY KEPT STARING AT
THE CHALK, BORED.**

The football player
owes me 25 cents,

•••

**BUT I HAVE A FEELING
I'M NEVER SEEING MY
QUARTER BACK.**

Why did the soccer player
pick up the cello?

•••

**HE WENT FROM MIDFIELDER
TO BIG FIDDLER.**

I saw the baseball player
on the back of a milk carton.

•••

**I GUESS HE NEVER
MADE IT HOME.**

Why was the lonely
lion ashamed?

•••

NO PRIDE.

We had a whole party
around the lion's head.

•••

IT WAS THE MANE THEME.

I wanted to talk about
my judgmental parents,

•••

**SO I SCHEDULED
DISAPPOINTMENT.**

My friend dressed up as
a mushroom for Halloween.

●●●

HE'S A REAL FUNGI.

Do you know why the button
is in such a bad mood?

•••

I THINK HE'S DE-PRESSED.

All the holiday spirits
failed their test.

•••

**ONLY THE GHOST
OF CHRISTMAS PASSED.**

I went to a great DC-comics convention.

•••

IT WAS MARVEL-LESS!

Where do astronauts keep their food?

•••

IN THEIR LAUNCH BOX.

My sommelier passed away
last month.

•••

**HE WAS SUCH A
GRAPE MAN.**

What's the most important
part of any Middle East
cabinet meeting?

•••

THE CENTER PEACE.

What is a pirate's favorite
fast-food restaurant?

•••

LONG JOHN SILVER'S.

I think I might be allergic
to my barista.

•••

**EVERY TIME I SEE HIM,
HE MAKES ME COUGHY.**

If Peter ever cooks the lost boys' breakfast

•••

- HE'LL BE A FRYING PAN.

My boss came to the bar with us.

•••

HE ORDERED EVERYONE AROUND.

When I don't wear glasses,
everyone looks smaller.

•••

MUST BE SHORT-SIGHTED.

I found a hilarious
new rock.

•••

**WHEN I THREW IT AT MY
WINDOW IT CRACKED UP.**

Working with fabrics
can make you sweat,

•••

**BUT WORKING WITH YARN
MAKES YOU SWEATER.**

How come Native Americans
so good at sneaking around?

•••

**THEY ALWAYS WALK
ON THEIR TIPI-TOES.**

I wanted to listen to
a Linkin Park cover band
from Nepal,

● ● ●

**BUT INDIAN IT DOESN'T
EVEN MATTER.**

Why did the cheerleader
ask for change?

● ● ●

**SHE WANTED
A QUARTER BACK.**

How did the dog ride
his bicycle?

•••

HE DOGGIE PADDLED.

Why was the big bad wolf
kicked out of Hogwarts?

•••

**HE THREATENED
TO HUFFLEPUFF.**

What did the big tomato
say to the little tomato?

...

KETCHUP.

What do you call a wrinkly
dog that glows in the dark?

•••

A SHARPIE.

My mom's sister is so cold,

•••

**WE CALL HER
AUNT ARCTICA.**

A bin might not stink up
your house,

●●●

BUT GARBAGE CAN.

The new exhibit had an
interesting security detail.

●●●

**IT WAS VERY
AVANT-GUARD.**

Did I tell you about the camping
trip we took to the reservoir?

•••

IT WAS VERY INTENTS.

What do you call a guy
who enjoys seizures?

•••

HAPPYLEPTIC.

The petting zoo has
some excellent gifts.

•••

**I GOT MY DAUGHTER
A NICE GOAT BAG.**

Did you hear about the cowboy
who couldn't afford a new car?

•••

HE SADDLED ON A HORSE.

What do you call spicy
Jewish bread?

•••

CHALLAHPEÑO.

It cost me an arm and a leg,

•••

**BUT I REALLY PULLED
OUT ALL THE STOPS
FOR THIS HALLOWEEN'S
PIRATE COSTUME.**

What do you can a lizard detective?

•••

INVESTIGATOR.

If I laugh every time
I feel nostalgic,

●●●

**IS IT BECAUSE I HAVE
A FUZZY MEMORY?**

A squirrel just stole
my testicles,

●●●

**THEN TOOK OFF IN MY CAR!
JUST THINKING ABOUT IT
DRIVES ME NUTS!**

Why do grapes cry
all the time?

•••

**THEY HAVE A LOT
TO WINE ABOUT.**

What do you get when you put together eight religious women and a priest named Bruce?

•••

NUN, NUN, NUN, NUN, NUN, NUN, NUN, NUN, BATMAN.

Choosing the materials for a tombstone

•••

IS A REALLY GRAVE MATTER.

Did you hear about the lawyer
who couldn't get a drink?

•••

HE PASSED THE BAR.

How do orcas prefer
their meat?

•••

WHALE-DONE.

What gift do you get
a blind Apple Genius?

•••

A SEEING IDOG.

I really hate the haircut
my barber gave me,

•••

IF I MAY BE SO BALD.

I took all the lead
out of my glasses.

•••

**NOW THEY'RE MUCH
EASIER ON THE EYES.**

If you mess up in
cheese-making school,

•••

**IT CAN GO ON YOUR
PARMESAN RECORD.**

My friend decided to measure his new yacht by feet.

•••

IT WAS SO WIDE HE ALMOST RAN OUT OF BREADTH.

There are a lot of similarities between the two characters,

•••

BUT IN THE END, A HOUSE IS NOT A HOLMES.

What did one football pig
say to the other?

•••

"STOP HOGGING THE BALL!"

Why do all pirates have
good eyesight?

•••

**THEY ARE ALL MEN
OF THE SEE.**

I have an irrational fear
of speed bumps,

● ● ●

**BUT I'M SLOWLY GETTING
OVER IT.**

What do you call the noise
a permanent marker makes?

● ● ●

A SHARP E.

What do you call the noise
a permanent marker makes?

•••

A SHARP E.

Why do they keep morays
at the power company?

•••

**THEY'RE GOOD AT PRODUCING
EELECTRICITY.**

Where do rich people go when they need a locksmith?

•••

THE FLORIDA KEYS.

What do you call a fish with car trouble?

•••

A TUNAP.

What do you call a
crime-solving mammal?

•••

AN AMATEUR SLOTH.

There wasn't a lot to eat at
the peanut butter convention,

•••

**BUT THEY PUT OUT
A NICE SPREAD.**

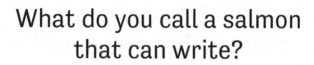

What do you call a salmon
that can write?

•••

A CALLIGRAFISH.

A guitar might be difficult
to put together,

•••

**BUT DRUMS ARE MUCH
EASIER TO A CYMBAL.**

When you can't let go of
your partner – that's love.

•••

**BUT WHEN SOMETHING BITES
YOU UNDERWATER AND DOESN'T
LET GO – THAT'S A MORAY.**

Why do pennies fall from
the sky all of a sudden?

•••

**BECAUSE OF CLIMATE
CHANGE.**

I can't recommend investing
in escalator companies.

•••

THEY'RE TOO UP AND DOWN.

Which playground ride is
the blind lumberjack's favorite?

•••

THE SEESAW.

When can you see two
palm trees kissing?

•••

WHEN THEY'RE ON A DATE.

Before it was carved out,

•••

**THE BEAUTY
OF MT. RUSHMORE
WAS UNPRESIDENTED.**

I'm not worried
about misplacing nails
in my toolshed.

•••

**I ALREADY KNOW
THE DRILL.**

The only way to learn brail

•••

IS THROUGH HANDS-ON EXPERIENCE.

I thought working as
a trash collector was gross.

•••

**BUT SELLING PRODUCE
IS GROCER.**

Did you hear about the
new Catholic pizza place?

•••

**THEIR BABY CHEEZUS
IS DIVINE!**

Do you remember the
chiropractor joke I told you?

•••

**IT WAS ABOUT
A WEEK BACK.**

To the actor who stole my
spot in the cast:

•••

**I HOPE YOU BREAK
A LEG.**

You should always pay
your exorcist.

•••

**YOU DON'T WANT TO GET
REPOSSESSED.**

What's the difference between a boulder and a rainbow?

•••

ONE IS REALLY HEAVY BUT THE OTHER IS PRETTY LIGHT.

I wonder if sick pharmaceutical reps

•••

GET A TASTE OF THEIR OWN MEDICINE.

I bet the first person who thought of cloning

●●●

JUST WANTED TO REINVENT THEMSELVES.

What did one lighter say to the other?

●●●

"YOU'RE NO MATCH FOR ME!"

What do you do when you
can't wrap your gift?

•••

**JUST MAKE IT
PRESENTABLE.**

Once you take the gloves
out of the package –

•••

**THERE'S NO
UNBOXING THEM.**

Reptiles will have a difficult
time getting through a wall,

•••

BUT A DINO MIGHT.

I cut onions in a restaurant kitchen.

•••

YOU COULD SAY IT'S PRETTY DICEY WORK.

Good poop jokes aren't my go-to humor...

•••

BUT THEY'RE A SOLID #2.

What's the most important
thing to have at
a housewarming party?

•••

ADDRESS.

I tried using my workout
routine for my password,

•••

**BUT IT WASN'T
STRONG ENOUGH.**

Took my cupcake
on the plane to London,

•••

**BUT WHEN WE ARRIVED
IT TURNED INTO
AN ENGLISH MUFFIN.**

My friend used to work
at the circus.

•••

**HE WAS A HUMAN
CANNONBALL WHEN
THEY FIRED HIM.**

I didn't like it when
my wife asked me to blow
cool air on her...

•••

BUT NOW I'M A FAN.

You can't move trees
in your car

•••

IF YOU HAVE A BIG TRUNK.

My wife says she can't
walk our new dog.

•••

**I SHOULD HAVE KNOWN –
SHE'S ALLERGIC TO GLUTEN,
AND HE'S PURE BREAD.**

"Why is this tea so sweet?"

•••

- "MY SUGAR DROPPED."

If you spend your mornings
in a German bakery,

•••

YOU'RE GOING TO HAVE
A GLUTEN MORGEN.

Why did the nurse
carry a red pen?

•••

**IN CASE SHE NEEDED
TO DRAW BLOOD.**

My friend has a phobia
of stairs...

•••

**HE'S AFRAID
IT'S ESCALATING.**

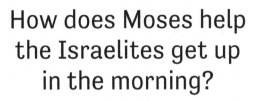

How does Moses help
the Israelites get up
in the morning?

•••

**HEBREWS THEM
SOME COFFEE.**

The invention of the nail
really helped

...

**TO HAMMER
EVERYTHING DOWN.**

Did you hear about the clock
that went to jail?

...

**IT TRIED TO HOLD UP
A MINUTE.**

Where does the wealthy
prospector keep his gold?

•••

"BUY THE RIVER" BANK.

I took a gig
tending horses.

•••

**IT'S NOT MUCH,
BUT IT'S A STABLE JOB.**

My friends asked me why
I was going to the gym if
I wanted to become a farmer.

•••

**I TOLD THEM I HAD TO WORK
ON MY CALVES.**

I painted the baby's room
before we knew the gender.

•••

**THAT'S LIFE – SOMETIMES
YOU GOTTA ROLL THE DYE
AND SEE WHAT COMES OUT.**

What type of doctor
is Dr. Pepper?

•••

A GENERAL FIZZY-CIAN.

Working at a stable can be
very calming.

•••

**YOU REALLY LEARN HOW
TO HOLD YOUR HORSES.**

Criminals always whisper
to each other...

•••

**BECAUSE WHAT THEY
DO ISN'T ALOUD.**

What do you call the sound
of a ripe nectarine?

•••

PEACH-PERFECT.

What do you call
a picnic with sour milk
and moldy bread?

•••

AN EXPIRATION DATE.

Who is the number one
best-selling romance
author of all time?

•••

PAIGE TURNER.

What do you get when you combine a washing machine with a dishwasher?

•••

I DON'T KNOW BUT IT'S GOING TO MAKE ONE CLEAN JOKE.

What's the fastest way to kill a diabetic?

•••

PUT A BOUNTY ON HIS HEAD.

I got mugged
while taking a bath...

•••

**HAD TO HAND OVER
MY ROBBER DUCK.**

They say that people
with one ear can't
enjoy music...

•••

**BUT THAT'S JUST
A STEREOTYPE.**

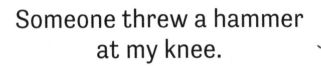

Someone threw a hammer
at my knee.

• • •

**IT WAS REALLY
THOR.**

I wanted to ask my barista to add ice cream to my coffee this morning...

•••

BUT AFFOGATO.

I was looking forward to the trip to the furniture store...

•••

BUT I COULDN'T WALK SOFA.

I'm always careful when
I'm around crabs...

•••

**I HEARD THEY'RE PRAWN
TO VIOLENCE.**

What did the blocked river
say to the well?

•••

"WELL, I'LL BE DAMMED."

It's a hard time
for cannibals.

•••

**MOST CAN'T AFFORD
TO LIVE HAND-TO-MOUTH
ANYMORE.**

What is the opposite
of a full room?

•••

AN ANTECHAMBER.

What is the best place
to hide a dad joke?

•••

UNDER THE SON.

What makes hunters
so good at sneaking?

•••

**THEY WEAR CLOTHES
MADE OF HIDE.**

People in glass houses

• • •

**SHOULD NOT LIVE
A STONE'S THROW AWAY
FROM EACH OTHER.**

The break-in at the zoo
sent the police

• • •

**ON A WILD
GOOSE CHASE.**

"Do you like party games?"

•••

- **"I DO, BUT I DRAW THE LINE AT PICTIONARY."**

What did the dad pastry
say to the son pastry?

•••

**I'M SORRY I WAS A WAFER
SO LONG.**

Where can you find a man
with no legs?

•••

**RIGHT WHERE
YOU LEFT HIM.**

How do lumberjacks
protect their passwords?

•••

THEY LOG OUT.

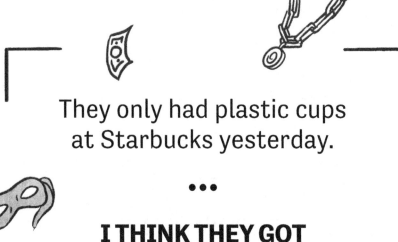

They only had plastic cups
at Starbucks yesterday.

•••

**I THINK THEY GOT
MUGGED.**

What do you give a janitor
on his birthday?

•••

**THROW HIM A
SUPPLIES PARTY.**

What do you get when
you cross a pronghorn
with a reindeer?

•••

**I DON'T KNOW, BUT YOU'LL
MAKE A QUICK BUCK.**

A woman was arrested for
a DUI. The judge asked her
if it was her first offense.

•••

**SHE REPLIED, "FIRST
OFFENSE, THEN A LAWN,
THEN A HOUSE."**

Why are dogs afraid
of clocks?

•••

**THEY ARE FULL
OF TICKS.**

Why did the yacht fall
into bad habits?

•••

PIER PRESSURE.

Why do Australian ambulance
drivers always come in twos?

•••

**BECAUSE THEY ARE TRAINED
PAIR-A-MEDICS.**

Where did the pound
and the kilogram meet?

●●●

MORNING MASS.

You should never jump
head-first into a colander.

●●●

**YOU'LL ONLY STRAIN
YOURSELF.**

To the person who stole
my anti-depressants –

•••

**I HOPE YOU ARE
HAPPY NOW!**

Why did the rapper
go to the farm?

•••

**TO GATHER SOME
FRESH BEATS.**

Why is November 24th
the best day to give up
an addiction?

•••

**YOU CAN QUIT
COLD TURKEY.**

Why was the amoeba
fired from the university
laboratory?

•••

**FOR BEING
UNCULTURED.**

My drinking habits are a lot
like my parenting habits.

•••

ABSINTH.

What kind of car would you
drive to a party in Norway?

•••

FJORD FIESTA.

I really thought
chiropractic was a hoax.

•••

**NOW I STAND
CORRECTED.**

What do you call two
monkeys that share
an Amazon account?

•••

PRIME MATES.

I tried signing up
as an organ donor,

•••

**BUT I DIDN'T HAVE
THE GUTS.**

How does Bigfoot
keep an eye on his kids?

•••

HE SASQ-WATCH.

I was looking for parking
yesterday but kept
missing a spot.

•••

**I JUST HAD A LOT
ON MY MIND.**

What do you call
an Irish lawn chair?

•••

PATTY O'FURNITURE.

How did the tackling
chicken cross the road?

•••

IT RAN A FOWL.

I saw someone post about
how they handled
their paranoia.

•••

**IT WAS INTERESTING,
SO I FOLLOWED THEM.**

Why is it so dangerous to go outside when it's raining cats and dogs?

•••

YOU MIGHT STEP IN A POODLE.

Why are mimes
the scariest?

•••

**BECAUSE THEY DO
UNSPEAKABLE THINGS.**

What's the most
embarrassing plant
to have on your face?

•••

EGGPLANT.

What's the heaviest
Asian dish in history?

•••

ONE-TON SOUP.

Three golf clubs walk into a bar.
The first one orders a beer.
The second one orders whiskey.

•••

**THE THIRD ONE SAYS,
"NOTHING FOR ME, THANKS.
I'M THE DRIVER."**

Why are computer programs
not appetizing?

•••

THEY'RE BYTE-SIZED.

What's the best thing
about vegan pâté
for lazy people?

•••

**YOU CAN GET IT
DE-LIVERED.**

What do morally ambiguous
cannibals prefer to eat?

•••

VEGETABLES.

My doctor told me
I was colorblind.

•••

**BOY, THAT NEWS CAME RIGHT
OUT OF THE ORANGE.**

My therapist asked me
if I'd solved my
possessions problem.

•••

I CAN'T SAY THAT I HAVE.

What do they call the Jerry
Springer Show in Germany?

•••

KINDER SURPRISE.

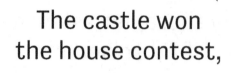

The castle won
the house contest,

•••

**BUT THERE WERE SOME
HONORABLE MANSIONS.**

What did one nut say to
the other as they separated?

•••

"CASHEW LATER!"

Never use the Titanic
as a conversation starter.

•••

**IT'S A TERRIBLE
ICEBREAKER.**

I found a place to get gas
for only two bucks!

•••

IT'S CALLED TACO BELL.

Why are dogs so good
at floating in the water?

•••

**BECAUSE THEY ARE
SUCH GOOD BUOYS.**

What do you call a hive
without any doors
or windows?

•••

UN-BEE-LIVABLE.

Did you hear about
the comedian telling jokes
about Vladimir Putin?

•••

**HIS MATERIAL WAS GOOD,
BUT HIS EXECUTION
WAS TERRIBLE.**

What do you call someone
who can't tell the difference
between wallpaper
and toilet paper?

•••

GROSS.

I don't know why my wife
keeps asking me which is the
northernmost state
in America...

•••

BUT ALASKA.

Did you hear about the stubborn
demolition expert?

•••

**HE KEPT BANGING HIS HEAD
AGAINST THE WALL.**

Do you know why
he stopped?

•••

**HE FINALLY HAD
A BREAKTHROUGH.**

Did you hear about the
two telecoms execs
that got married?

•••

**THEIR SERVICE WASN'T
VERY GOOD, BUT THE
RECEPTION WAS EXCELLENT.**

I came home to find my wife
had been on eBay all day.

•••

**SO I LOWERED
MY ASKING PRICE.**

What do you call a superhero who helps strangers out of the kindness of his heart?

•••

A DAD.

All jokes aside, it is our dream to bring joy to our readers. A short review on Amazon can go a long way in helping us do just that. You can scan this QR code to access our review page and leave us your thoughts on the worst dad jokes for the best dads:

Made in the USA
Las Vegas, NV
18 December 2023